Countries of the World

Russia

by Kristin Thoennes

Consultant:
Oleg V. Stepanov
Vice Consul
Consulate General of the
Russian Federation in San Francisco

Bridgestone Books

an imprint of Capstone Press
Mankato, Minnesota

Bridgestone Books are published by Capstone Press
818 North Willow Street, Mankato, Minnesota 56001
http://www.capstone-press.com

Library of Congress Cataloging-in-Publication Data
Thoennes, Kristin.
  Russia/by Kristin Thoennes.
  p. cm. (Countries of the world)
  Includes bibliographical references and index.
  Summary: Discusses the landscape, culture, food, animals, and sports of Russia.
  ISBN 0-7368-0156-1
  1. Russia (Federation)—Juvenile literature. [1. Russia (Federation)] I. Title. II. Series. III. Series:
Countries of the world (Mankato, Minn.)
DK510.23.T49 1999
947—dc21
                                                                                          98-41777
                                                                                                 CIP
                                                                                                  AC

Editorial Credits
Blanche R. Bolland, editor; Timothy Halldin, cover designer; Linda Clavel and Timothy Halldin, illustrators;
   Kimberly Danger and Sheri Gosewisch, photo researchers

Photo Credits
Jean S. Buldain, 5 (bottom), 16
Maxine Cass, 8
Photri-Microstock, 10; Frank Siteman, 18
StockHaus Limited, 5 (top)
Tom Stack & Associates/Mark Newman, 6; Thomas Kitchin, 14; J. Lotter, 20
Valan Photos/Christine Osborne, cover; Fred Bruemmer, 12

Table of Contents

Fast Facts

Name: Russian Federation

Capital: Moscow

Population: About 148 million

Language: Russian

Religion: Mostly Russian Orthodox

Size: 6,592,800 square miles (17,075,352 square kilometers)

Russia is almost as big as the United States and Canada combined.

Crops: Grains, potatoes, sugar beets

Maps

ALASKA

Arctic Ocean

Pacific Ocean

FINLAND

ESTONIA

LATVIA St. Petersburg

BELARUS

Moscow

UKRAINE

Black Sea

Caspian Sea

KAZAKHSTAN

MONGOLIA

CHINA

Ural Mountains

Volga River

Lena River

Amur River

Lake Baikal

Russia

▲ Mountains

Russia

Flag

The Russian flag has three horizontal stripes. The stripes are white, blue, and red. White means pure. Blue stands for noble. Red means bold and brave. The flag of the Russian Federation was first used by the Russian Empire from 1699 to 1918. At that time, each stripe stood for a branch of the armed forces. Russia adopted this flag when it became a country in 1991.

Currency

The unit of currency in Russia is the ruble. One hundred kopecks make up 1 ruble.

In the late 1990s, about 6 rubles equaled 1 U.S. dollar. About 4 rubles equaled 1 Canadian dollar.

The Land

Russia was part of the Soviet Union until 1991. Russia now is a member of the Commonwealth of Independent States.

Russia is the largest country in the world. Most of Russia lies in Asia. The Ural (YOOR-al) Mountains divide Asian and European Russia.

Russia has three types of land. The treeless tundra covers the far north. The ground in this flat plain stays frozen most of the time. The taiga (TYE-gah) is south of the tundra. Large evergreen forests cover the taiga. The steppe lies south of the taiga. This flat grassland is dry and has few trees.

Russia's Lake Baikal is the world's oldest and deepest lake. The Caspian Sea in the southwest is the world's largest inland sea. Russia's Lena River is the longest river in Europe. The Volga in central Russia is Asia's longest river.

The tundra meets the mountains in the northeast.

Life at Home

Life in Russia has changed since the breakup of the Soviet Union. Most people used to live in the country. But about 75 percent of Russians now live in crowded cities.

In cities, most families live in tall apartment buildings. The apartments are small. Children, parents, and grandparents often live together. Russians call their grandmothers "babushkas" (bah-BOOSH-kahs). Babushkas sometimes shop for the family and care for their grandchildren.

Many Russians own country homes. They spend vacations and weekends at these dachas (DAH-chahs). Dachas often are small, plain houses. Russians grow vegetables on the land by their dachas.

Most people in Russian villages live in small wooden or brick houses. Villagers often work on nearby farms.

Country houses usually are wooden.

Going to School

Russian children start school at age 6 or 7. Children learn reading, writing, and math. They also study history, geography, science, and languages. Many students choose to learn English.

Russian children go to school six days each week. The school day ends around two o'clock. Teachers give a lot of homework.

Teachers in Russia do not give letter grades. They grade tests and homework with the numbers one through five. Five is the highest grade.

Russians must attend school for 10 years. Students take a test after each grade. The test after eighth grade decides which kind of high school children will attend.

Russia has schools for children with special talents. Some schools teach ballet. The actions tell a story in this graceful kind of dance. Other schools teach acting, languages, or music.

Students listen to spoken English to learn the language.

Russian Food

Farmers on Russia's steppes grow grain. Russians use grain in many of their common foods. Bread is an important food in Russia. Russians eat more rye bread than people in any other country. Kasha (KAH-shah) is a cooked grain. Russians eat kasha with butter.

Russians eat soup at most meals. One common soup is borsch (BOORSH). The beets in borsch give the soup a red-pink color. A cabbage soup called shchi (SHEE) is another favorite.

Russians eat many foods with sour cream. They put sour cream on borsch. They also put sour cream on blini (blee-NEE). Some people eat these thin pancakes with jam.

Caviar (KAH-vee-ahr) is a famous Russian treat. These tiny fish eggs taste salty. People around the world prize black caviar from sturgeon in Russia's Caspian Sea.

Cabbage is a popular vegetable in Russia.

13

Clothes

Most Russian clothes look like clothes that North Americans wear. But Russians sometimes dress as people did long ago. They often wear this traditional clothing on special occasions. The clothes remind the Russians of their history.

Russians sew fancy patterns on traditional clothes. These oberegi (ob-er-EG-ih) decorations appear on cuffs, hems, and collars. Some Russians believe oberegi decorations keep away evil spirits.

People in cold northern Russia need warm clothing. They wear fur coats and hats. The fur might be from foxes, ermines, or mink. The hats cover most of the head and neck.

Other kinds of headwear also are popular in Russia. Many girls wear large bows in their hair. Babushkas wrap head scarves over their hair. They tie the scarves under the chin. Some North Americans call these scarves babushkas.

Traditional Russian clothing has oberegi decorations.

Animals

Many animals live in the forests of Russia's taiga region. Sables, ermines, and mink are small animals. Larger animals in this area include the polar fox, silver fox, and elk.

Other animals live in southeastern Russia. Black bears make their homes in dens there. Amur (ah-MYUR) tigers and Amur leopards live in the forests and grasslands. These animals were named for a river. The Amur River flows between Russia and China.

Lake Baikal is home to nerpas. These freshwater seals do not live anywhere else in the world.

Only a few animals can live in the tundra. Cold conditions make it hard for animals to find food and water. Polar bears, reindeer, and arctic foxes like the cold. Seals and walruses swim in the sea north of the tundra.

The Amur leopard is named for a Russian river.

Sports and Games

Russians enjoy playing and watching many sports. Soccer is the most popular sport in Russia. Other favorites include gymnastics, track and field, and basketball.

Many Russians skate and play ice hockey in winter. Russian figure skaters often win medals at the Olympic Games.

Chess is a popular board game in Russia. Chess involves moving pieces to capture the other player's pieces. People in Russia often play chess in parks. Many Russians enjoy watching chess matches. Children begin to learn chess in the first grade.

People in certain parts of Russia enjoy other sports. Reindeer sled racing is popular in the north. People in southeastern Russia canoe on the Amur River.

Figure skating is popular in Russia.

Holidays

Russians throw parties and give gifts on New Year's Day. They also ice skate, dance, and take sleigh rides.

Russians welcome spring during Shrovetide. This celebration comes seven weeks before Easter. Shrovetide lasts seven days. People make noise and play tricks. They go sledding and have snowball fights.

Easter is an important religious holiday in Russia. Russians paint eggs with wax and bright dyes. They eat special Easter cakes and cookies.

Victory Day on May 9 marks the end of World War II (1939-1945). Russians remain silent for one minute. This silence honors those who died in the war. Russians then dance and sing.

Russians celebrate Independence Day on June 12. Russia broke away from the Soviet Union on this date in 1991.

Russians give painted eggs as Easter presents.

Hands On: Play the Bear Game

The bear is a favorite animal in Russia. The bear stands for strength and knowledge. You can play a game that features a bear.

<u>What You Need</u>

Chalk   6 or more players

<u>What You Do</u>

1. Use the chalk to mark off a small area for the bear's den.
2. Choose one player to be the bear. The bear stands in the den. The other players walk around outside the den.
3. Have the bear shout, "The bear is coming." The bear then tries to catch the other players. When the bear taps another player, that person also becomes a bear.
4. The bears return to the den. They join hands and repeat step 3. Continue until all the players except one are bears. This player is the winner.

Learn to Speak Russian

The Russian language uses a different alphabet than the English language. This Cyrillic (suh-RIHL-ik) alphabet has 33 letters.

good-bye	До свидания	(da-svee-DAHN-yah)
hello	Эдравствуйте	(zdrahst-VOO-yeh-teh)
no	Нет	(NHET)
please	Пожалуйста	(poh-JAH-lys-tah)
thank you	Спасибо	(spah-SEE-bah)
yes	Да	(DA)

Words to Know

ballet (BAL-lay)—a performance that uses dancc to tell a story; many famous ballet dancers come from Russia.
beet (BEET)—a red root vegetable; Russians make borsch from beets.
cabbage (KAB-ij)—a leafy vegetable with green or purple leaves; Russians make shchi from cabbage.
taiga (TYE-gah)—a forest with mainly evergreen trees
tundra (TUHN-dra)—a treeless area of frozen soil in the far north

Read More

Arnold, Helen. *Russia.* Postcards from. Austin, Texas: Raintree Steck-Vaughn, 1996.

Bickman, Connie. *Russia.* Through the Eyes of Children. Edina, Minn.: Abdo & Daughters, 1994.

Useful Addresses and Internet Sites

Embassy of the Russian Federation
1125 16th Street NW
Washington, DC 20036

Embassy of the Russian Federation
52 Range Road
Ottawa, ON K1N 8JB
Canada

ABC Country Book of Russia
http://www.theodora.com/wfb/russia_geography.html
The Official Guide to Russia
http://www.interknowledge.com/russia

Index

INCREDIBLE SPACE

Spacecraft

by Steve Kortenkamp

Reading Consultant:
Barbara J. Fox
Reading Specialist
North Carolina State University

Capstone
press®

Mankato, Minnesota

Blazers is published by Capstone Press,
151 Good Counsel Drive, P.O. Box 669, Mankato, Minnesota 56002.
www.capstonepress.com

Library of Congress Cataloging-in-Publication Data
Kortenkamp, Steve.
    Spacecraft/by Steve Kortenkamp.
    p. cm. — (Blazers. Incredible space)
    Includes bibliographical references and index.
    Summary: "Discusses information about spacecraft within recent years as well as the future of
spacecraft" — Provided by publisher.
    ISBN-13: 978-1-4296-2325-4 (hardcover)
    ISBN-10: 1-4296-2325-X (hardcover)
    1. Space vehicles — Juvenile literature. I. Title.
TL793.K662 2009
629.4 — dc22   2008029845

Editorial Credits
Abby Czeskleba, editor; Ted Williams, designer; Jo Miller, photo researcher

Photo Credits
Alamy/PHOTOTAKE Inc./Michael Carroll, 7
ESA, 10
NASA, 9, 12, 13, 15, 16–17, 24, 25, 27, 28–29, cover; John Hopkins University Applied Physics
    Laboratory/Southwest Research Institute, 19; JPL, 5; JPL-Caltech/University of Arizona, 23
Shutterstock/argus (technology background), throughout; hcss5 (minimal code background
    vector), throughout
SOHO, 21

1 2 3 4 5 6 14 13 12 11 10 09

Table of Contents

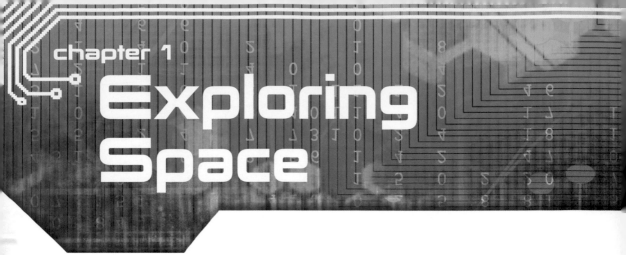

chapter 1
Exploring Space

The *Voyager 1* spacecraft silently flies through space. It is about the size of a car.

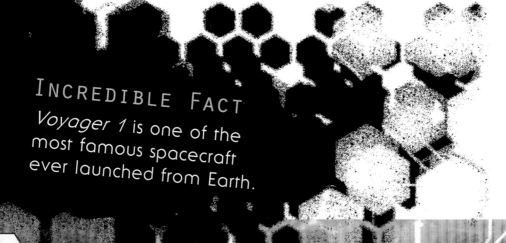

INCREDIBLE FACT
Voyager 1 is one of the most famous spacecraft ever launched from Earth.

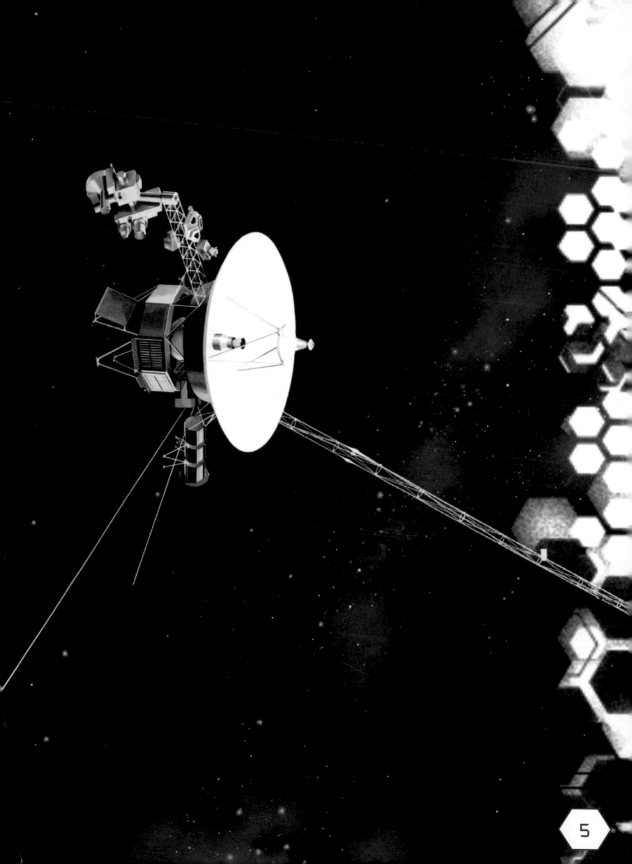

Voyager 1 and *Voyager 2* have traveled to many **planets**. They have explored Jupiter, Saturn, Uranus, and Neptune. Someday, they may explore more than just planets.

planet
a large object that moves around a star

Voyager 2 flies near Neptune.

chapter 2

Astronauts or Robots?

Many kinds of spacecraft explore space. Robotic spacecraft are called space probes. They carry computers and cameras. Some probes are big enough to carry smaller probes.

INCREDIBLE FACT

The two *Voyager* spacecraft are space probes.

The *Venus Express* flies near Venus.

Space probes explore places that are too dangerous for **astronauts**. Venus is too hot for astronauts to visit. But space probes have landed on Venus.

astronaut
a person who is trained to live and work in space

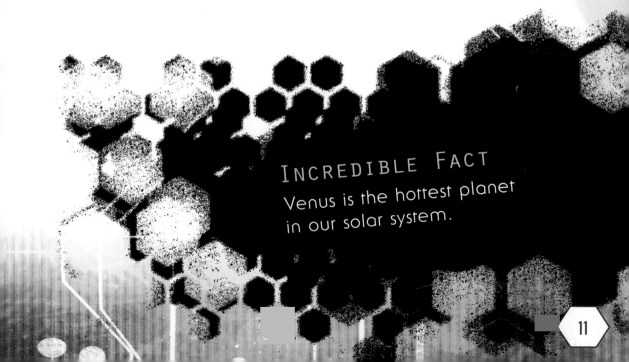

INCREDIBLE FACT
Venus is the hottest planet in our solar system.

The space shuttle *Atlantis* takes off into space.

Space shuttles are one type of spacecraft that carry astronauts. Astronauts can travel in spacecraft to explore places like the Moon.

space shuttle

a spacecraft that carries astronauts into space and back to Earth

A space shuttle lands after its mission.

The *International Space Station* (*ISS*) is a special kind of spacecraft. Astronauts live and work on the *ISS*. It has a bedroom, bathroom, and an exercise room.

International Space Station
a place for astronauts to live and work in space

Astronauts work on the
International Space Station.

Diagram

Earth

International
Space Station

astronaut

chapter 3
Probes to Fire and Ice

Scientists launched the *New Horizons* probe in 2006. The probe left Earth traveling more than 35,000 miles (56,327 kilometers) per hour.

INCREDIBLE FACT

The *New Horizons* probe should reach ice-cold Pluto by 2015.

Other probes may explore the Sun. The Sun has giant, exploding flames. Scientists want to learn how the Sun makes these flames.

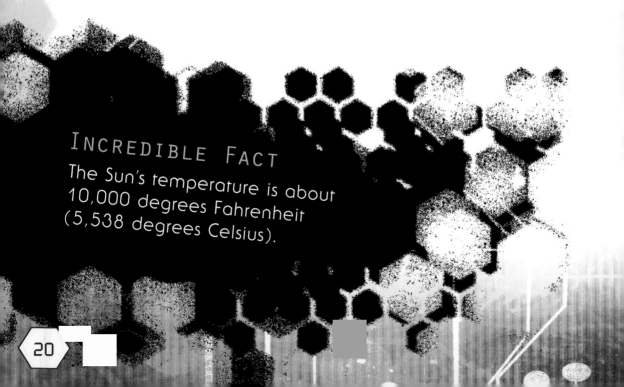

INCREDIBLE FACT
The Sun's temperature is about 10,000 degrees Fahrenheit (5,538 degrees Celsius).

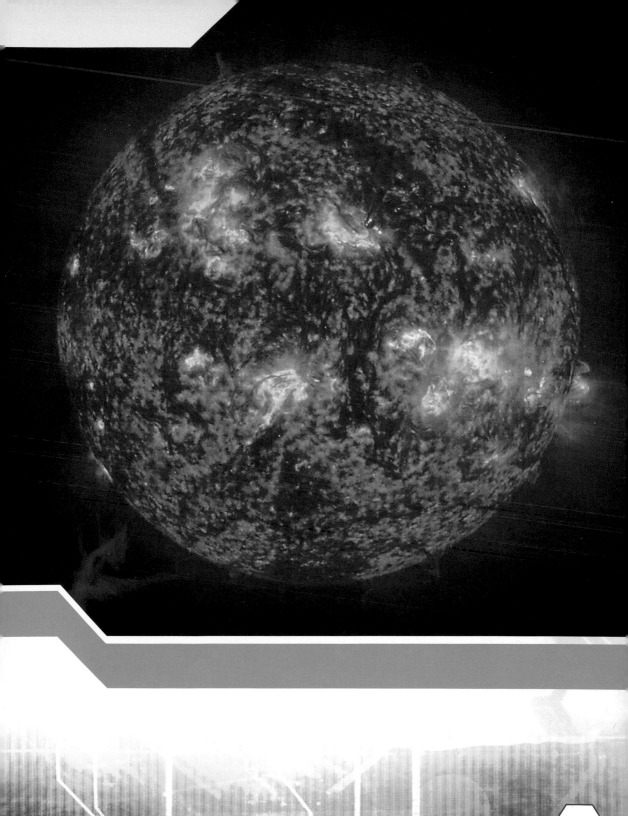

chapter 4
To Mars and the Stars

Probes on Mars have found safe places for people to live. One day, astronauts may travel to Mars to search for **Martian** life.

Martian

something on or from the planet Mars

INCREDIBLE FACT

The trip to Mars will be more than 150 million miles (241 million kilometers) long.

Astronauts and robots will explore Mars together.

Astronauts will live in a space station on Mars. They will explore Mars for two years before returning to Earth.

Space probes have explored every planet in our **solar system**. They may explore faraway **stars** in the future. What do you think the space probes will find?

solar system
the Sun and everything that circles it

star
a ball of hot, bright gases in space

The *Cassini* spacecraft drops a probe onto a moon of Saturn.

Traveling through Space

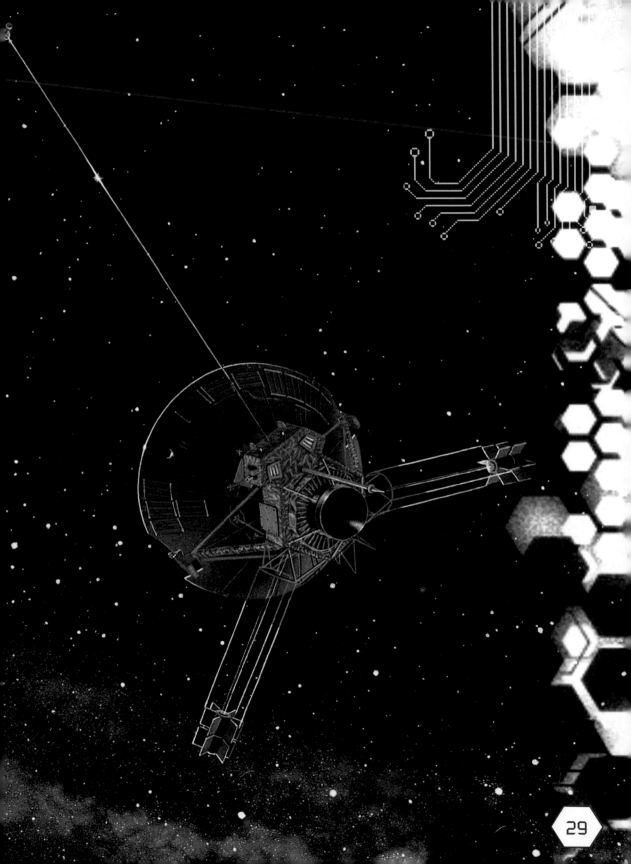

Glossary

astronaut (AS-truh-nawt) — a person who is trained to live and work in space

International Space Station (in-tur-NASH-uh-nuhl SPAYSS STAY-shuhn) — a place for astronauts to live and work in space

Martian (MAHR-shuhn) — something on or from the planet Mars

moon (MOON) — an object that moves around a bigger object in space

planet (PLAN-it) — a large object that moves around a star

solar system (SOH-lur SISS-tuhm) — the Sun and everything that circles it

space shuttle (SPAYSS SHUT-ul) — a spacecraft that carries astronauts into space and back to Earth

star (STAR) — a ball of hot, bright gases in space

Read More

Kortenkamp, Steve. *Space Probes.* The Solar System. Mankato, Minn.: Capstone Press, 2008.

Kortenkamp, Steve. *Space Shuttles.* The Solar System. Mankato, Minn.: Capstone Press, 2008.

Zuehlke, Jeffrey. *The Space Shuttle.* Pull Ahead Books. Minneapolis: Lerner, 2007.

Internet Sites

FactHound offers a safe, fun way to find educator-approved Internet sites related to this book.

Here's what you do:

1. Visit *www.facthound.com*
2. Choose your grade level.
3. Begin your search.

This book's ID number is 9781429623254.

FactHound will fetch the best sites for you!

Index

DATE DUE